WHO AM I?

SHIGERU MIYAMOTO:
I CREATED MARIO™

THOMAS KINGSLEY TROUPE

T0390206

Mitchell Lane
PUBLISHERS

Parent and Caregiver Tips for Creating Nonfiction Readers

The high-interest topics in the *Who Am I?* series are sure to get your young reader excited about reading nonfiction. While exploring a fascinating subject, your reader will be introduced to new concepts, facts, ideas, and vocabulary.

Tips for Reading Nonfiction

Talk about Nonfiction

Explain that nonfiction books provide facts about real-world topics. When readers read nonfiction, they gain a rich understanding of the world. They build background knowledge that provides a foundation for learning and academic success.

Look at the Parts

This book contains the following helpful features. Share the purpose of each feature with your reader.

Photos, Captions, and Graphic Aids

The photos, captions, maps, diagrams, time lines, and other graphic aids in nonfiction texts contain a wealth of information. Help your reader identify different ways information can be displayed.

Sidebars

These extra tidbits of information help satisfy readers' curiosity and expand their knowledge.

Table of Contents

Located at the front of the book, this list shows the big ideas within the text and the page numbers where they can be found.

Glossary

Located at the back of the book, the glossary defines key words and phrases that are related to the topic. These words and phrases can be found in the text in colored type.

Comprehension Questions (Fact Check)

Multiple-choice questions help readers self-check to make sure they understand what they read.

Index

Located at the back of the book, the index is an alphabetical list of topics and the page numbers where they can be found.

With a little help and guidance, your reader will be on their way to enjoying and learning from nonfiction books.

Mitchell Lane

PUBLISHERS

mitchelllanepub.com

2001 SW 31st Avenue
Hallandale, FL 33009

First Edition, 2025.
Author: Thomas Kingsley Troupe
Designer: Rhea Magaro
Editor: Kim Thompson

Series: Who Am I?
Title: Shigeru Miyamoto: I Created Mario / by Thomas Kingsley Troupe
Hallandale, FL : Mitchell Lane Publishers, [2025]

Library bound ISBN: 979-8-89260-253-2
Paperback ISBN: 979-8-89260-442-0
eBook ISBN: 979-8-89260-258-7

PHOTO CREDITS
Associated Press: Casey Curry/Invision, 22; Alamy: Image Press Agency, cover, 1; WENN Rights Ltd, 8; Arcade Images: p. 12, 19; Peregrine, 14; Andrew Cline, 16; Keith Homan, 17; pumpkinpie, 18; United Archives Gmbh, 20; SipaUSA, 21; PAImages, 23; James Anderson, 25; Shutterstock: Halyna Bihus, 1, 10; Miguel Lagoa, 4; Kuroyukihime, 5, 15, 29; USA-Pyon, 6; Eric Broder Von Dyke, 6; PatiPati 7; Studio_s, 8; Tutatamafilm, 9; Poetra. RH, 11; Jean Andrian, 12-13; Luciano Marques, 17, Mas_Geon, 20; New Africa, 21; PeopleImages.com, 24; ProStock, 26; Gorodenkoff, 27; Wikipedia: 10, 11,

CONTENTS

LET'S-A GO!

He wears suspenders, white gloves, and a red hat. His brother wears the same getup, but in green. Eating a mushroom makes him twice as tall. He drops down pipes and lives to collect coins. Who is this funny little guy?

We're talking about the world's most famous plumber—Mario, of course! He's the star of the enormous Mario Bros.® video game **franchise** owned by the Japanese company Nintendo. For more than 40 years, Mario and his Mushroom Kingdom friends have been adored by people around the globe.

The tiny Italian plumber has jumped his way to superstardom. Mario has appeared in over 200 video games. His face decorates all kinds of products. There are Mario toys, cereals, and T-shirts. Mario has starred in cartoons and board games. You can even buy a Mario toilet plunger!

MARCH
10

Creator Corner
March 10th is known as Mario Day because *Mar10* looks like *Mario* spelled out. On this day, fans around the world celebrate the coin-collecting plumber.

Mario fans are everywhere. They play his video games, dress up like him for Halloween, and recite his catchphrases. Where did this powered-up character come from? Who started all this?

MEET MIYAMOTO

Shigeru Miyamoto created Mario. He was born on November 16, 1952, in Sonobe, a small town near Kyoto, Japan. His parents were artists. They encouraged him to be creative and use his imagination. As a child, Miyamoto spent time exploring the outdoors, drawing, and playing baseball. His family didn't own a TV until he was 11 years old.

Miyamoto watched animated shows on TV. He quickly became interested in manga. In high school, he joined a manga club. He was inspired by the dynamic characters he saw and the artistry used to create them. He knew then that he wanted to become an artist.

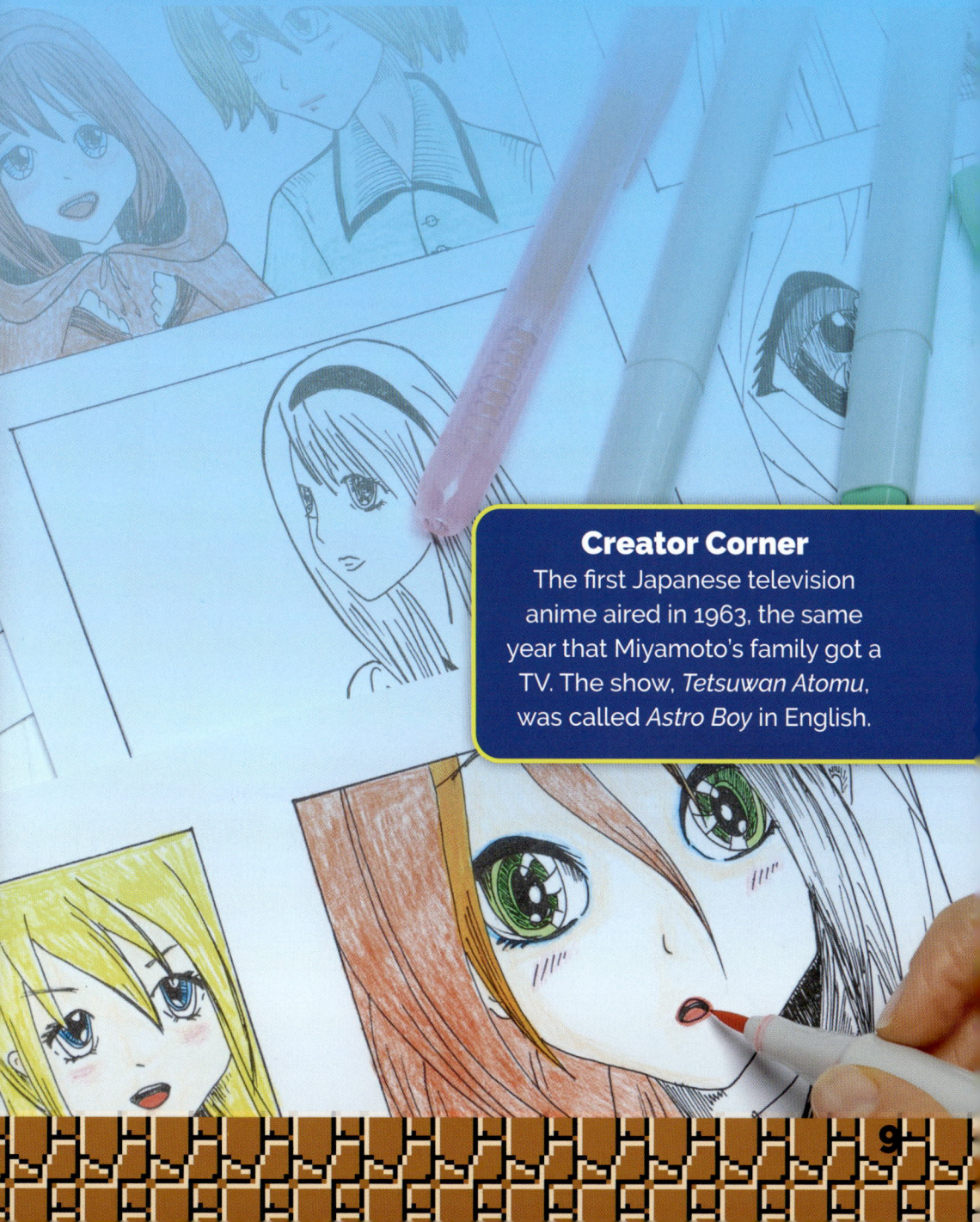

Creator Corner
The first Japanese television anime aired in 1963, the same year that Miyamoto's family got a TV. The show, *Tetsuwan Atomu*, was called *Astro Boy* in English.

Miyamoto's family moved to Kyoto. In the city, more opportunities were available to him. He attended Kanazawa College of Art. In 1977, he graduated with a degree in **industrial design**.

Miyamoto planned to be a manga artist, but his path took a different turn. A friend of his father got him a job interview at a company called Nintendo. Miyamoto got a position there working as a product designer.

Kanazawa College of Art

Creator Corner

Nintendo was founded in 1889. For many years, it made hand-painted playing cards. It later developed toys, board games, and video games.

PIPE DREAMS

In 1979, Nintendo released a space-themed **arcade** game called *Radar Scope*. The game was popular in Japan, so the company wanted to sell it to arcades in the United States. It took months for the shipments to arrive in the U.S. By then, the game was old news.

A lot of unused *Radar Scope* game cabinets were left. Nintendo wanted to use them for a new game based on the same technology. The company asked its designers for ideas. At the time, Miyamoto was working on a game that featured the cartoon character Popeye the Sailor.

Miyamoto suggested a Popeye arcade game. He made a sample game inspired by construction sites. Brutus, Popeye's enemy, pushed barrels off platforms to try and hit the hero. People at Nintendo liked the **gameplay**, but they didn't like how the characters looked on the screen.

Creator Corner

Where did the name Donkey Kong come from? Miyamoto imagined that the character was stubborn like a donkey. He took the name Kong from the giant ape who first appeared in a *King Kong* movie in 1933.

Miyamoto changed Brutus to an ape he named Donkey Kong. That became the game's name too. Popeye changed into a small construction worker in overalls that Miyamoto named Mr. Video. To help Mr. Video avoid dangers, a jump button was added. *Donkey Kong* arcade games arrived in America in 1981. The English instructions for the game gave Mr. Video a different name: Jumpman.

Donkey Kong was a hit in arcades. A sequel, *Donkey Kong Jr.*, followed in 1982. In this game, Jumpman's name changed to Mario. Oddly enough, Mario was the villain in *Donkey Kong Jr.*

Mario moved away from apes in 1983 when the two-player arcade game *Mario Bros.* was released. It introduced Mario's brother Luigi.

A home gaming **console**, the Nintendo Entertainment System, went on sale in the U.S. in 1985. It became wildly popular. A *Super Mario Bros.* video game **cartridge** came with the system.

POWERED-UP PLUMBER

Super Mario Bros. was a smashing success. People loved running Mario through levels and knocking Koopas off platforms. Mushrooms in the game turned ordinary Mario into Super Mario.

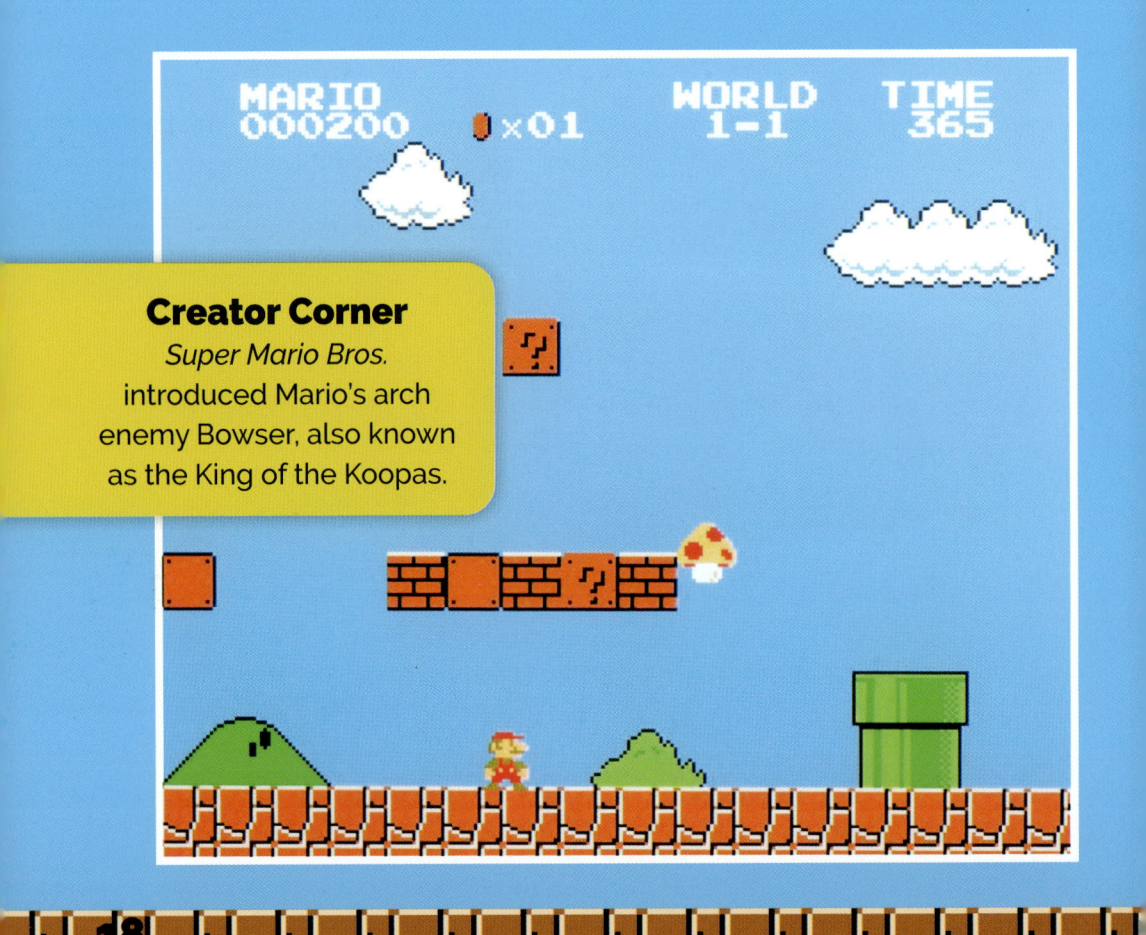

Creator Corner

Super Mario Bros. introduced Mario's arch enemy Bowser, also known as the King of the Koopas.

Miyamoto became Nintendo's top game designer. He brought many more creations to life. *The Legend of Zelda*, first released in 1986, was inspired by Miyamoto's experience exploring a cave as a child. A fox shrine in Kyoto, Japan, gave him the idea for *Star Fox*.

The live-action film *Super Mario Bros.* came to theaters in 1993. It was not a big success. People said it didn't capture the magic of Miyamoto's characters.

Thirty years later, *The Super Mario Bros. Movie* hit the big screen in 2023. This film was co-produced by Miyamoto and animated by Illumination Entertainment. Fans loved it. The movie made over a billion dollars worldwide and was nominated for many awards.

IT'S-A ME, MIYAMOTO!

Many people consider Miyamoto the greatest video game designer of all time. He explains that he wants his games to give players a different experience. "For us," he said, "the most important thing in making a game is that we make a game that's unique—something that no one else has created."

Because of his imagination and creativity, Miyamoto is often compared to Walt Disney and filmmaker Steven Spielberg. It's a compliment that Miyamoto doesn't like. He said, "It's everybody, and everybody at Nintendo as part of Nintendo creating this product." He doesn't feel it's fair to take all the credit.

Miyamoto receiving an award in 2010

Creator Corner

When he's creating games, Miyamoto often thinks about things he enjoyed as a child. For designing three-dimensional games, he remembers making puppets and using them to put on shows.

Miyamoto has been at Nintendo for over 45 years. He still works there today, finding ways to expand Nintendo and bring his creations to the world.

Over the years, Miyamoto has seen video games change—from arcade games and gaming consoles to handheld games, virtual reality games, and beyond. For each gaming experience, he has found ways for players to have extraordinary adventures.

Mario, his friends, and even his enemies, are lighthearted and fun. Jumping through the Mushroom Kingdom reminds people of the power of imagination.

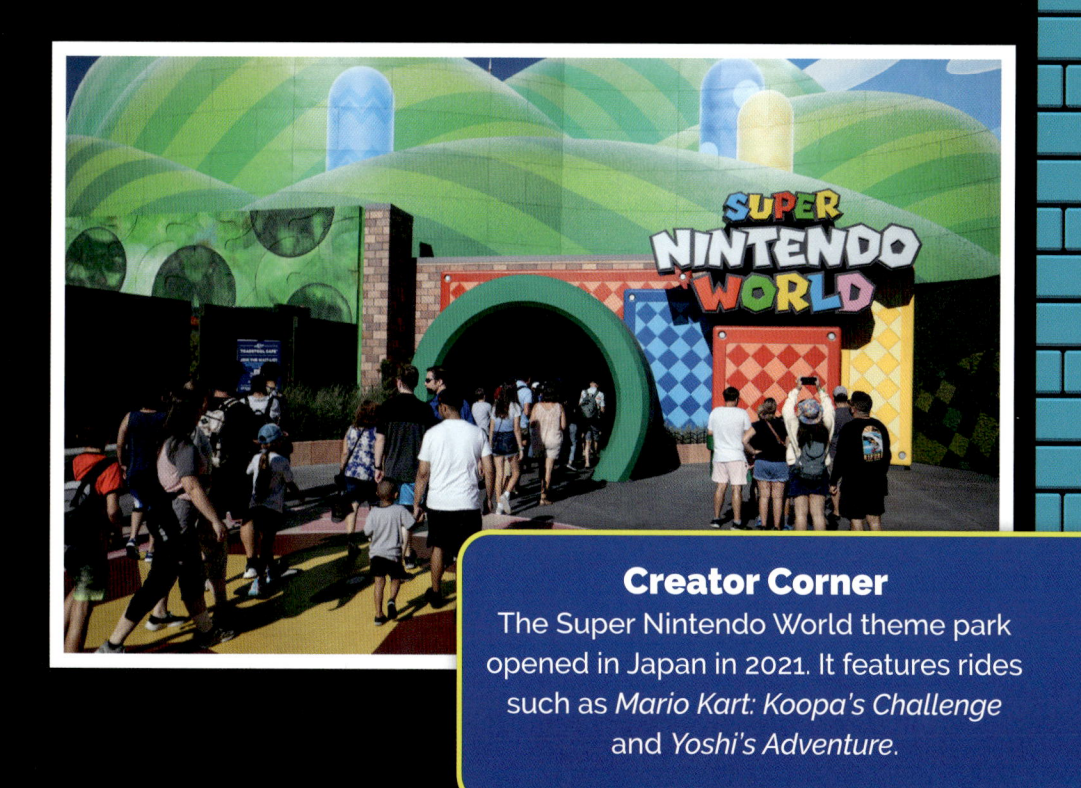

Creator Corner
The Super Nintendo World theme park opened in Japan in 2021. It features rides such as *Mario Kart: Koopa's Challenge* and *Yoshi's Adventure*.

BE A CREATOR

Inventing a unique video game character may seem tough, but it doesn't have to be. Every great success starts with a small idea. Miyamoto took things he loved, such as manga and nature, and combined them with his passion for art.

Miyamoto was asked to give advice for future video game creators. He said, "You have to be willing to show a game that you've created to other people and then hear their criticisms. Sometimes that can cause a lot of frustration for you."

Think about a character you would like to join on an adventure. Are they funny? Talented? How would they respond in different situations? Make sketches of your character. Learn to use animation software to bring them to life. With hard work and patience, a new video game legend will be born!

TIME LINE: SHIGERU MIYAMOTO AND MARIO

1952 Shigeru Miyamoto is born in Sonobe, Japan.

1963 After his family buys a TV, Miyamoto discovers anime and cartoons based on manga.

1977 Miyamoto graduates from Kanazawa College of Art. He begins working at Nintendo as a product designer.

1981 *Donkey Kong* comes to arcades in the United States.

1983 *Mario Bros.* is released, introducing Mario's brother Luigi.

1985 The Nintendo Entertainment System (NES) invades American homes; it includes *Super Mario Bros.*

1986 Miyamoto creation *The Legend of Zelda* is released.

1993 The live-action film *Super Mario Bros.* shows in theaters.

1996 *Super Mario 64* is released along with the Nintendo 64 console.

2019 The Japanese government names Miyamoto a Person of Cultural Merit.

2021 The Super Nintendo World theme park opens in Osaka, Japan.

2023 *The Super Mario Bros. Movie* is released in theaters.

GLOSSARY

arcade (ahr-KADE)
a business that has entertaining machines, such as pinball machines and video games, that you pay to use

artistry (AHR-tuh-stree)
the ability to make valuable and beautiful things

cartridge (KAHR-trij)
a case that holds a circuit chip containing a computer program and that is designed to insert into a machine that can read the program

console (KAHN-sole)
an electronic device for playing video games

dynamic (dye-NAM-ik)
full of life and energy; constantly changing

franchise (FRAN-chize)
a series of related works of art that include the same characters or characters in the same fictional universe

gameplay (GAME-play)
the way in which the action of a game occurs or is experienced

industrial design (in-DUHS-tree-uhl di-ZINE)
the practice of combining art, business, and engineering to plan and design products that will be made in a factory and sold in stores

manga (MAHNG-guh)
a style of comic books and graphic novels created and popularized in Japan

shrine (shrine)
a place that is regarded as holy and that is associated with a sacred person or relic